THE WORK-SHY

Wesleyan Poetry

THE

BLUNT RESEARCH GROUP

WORK-SHY

Wesleyan University Press   Middletown, Connecticut

NE TRAVAILLEZ JAMAIS

—Situationist slogan

CONTENTS

LOST
PRIVILEGE
COMPANY

The following poems operate under a strict constraint: they are composed entirely of phrases drawn from case files of inmates in the earliest youth prisons in California between 1910 and 1925. The original case files vary in length from 15 to 25 single-space typed pages. The histories contained in these files were gathered and archived by the now defunct Eugenics Records Office, an American organization that helped to shape the international eugenics movement through activities carried out in these reformatories (primarily at the Whittier State School, founded in 1891). Youths were incarcerated, according to Chicana scholar Miroslava Chavez-Garcia, for "evidence of incorrigibility, such as begging, hanging out with immoral companions, wandering the streets late at night after curfew, petty theft, and engaging in unsanctioned sexual activity."

Eugenics "researchers" and "fieldworkers" used these juvenile prisons—surrounded by the utopian fantasies of early California development—as laboratories to develop diagnostic procedures intended to identify "ungovernable" teens as mental "defectives" and to construct genealogies of "degenerate" families. These diagnoses were then used to determine whether the "propositus" (the teen "ward" in the case file) should be recommended for compulsory sterilization—to prevent him or her from "procreating"—a policy legalized by the California legislature in 1909 and pursued with great vigor until the early 1940s. Over 20,000 people were sterilized in California during this period, and some of the teens in these poems were referred to the sterilization "mills" of the Sonoma State Home and the Pacific Colony for the Feebleminded.

The development of eugenics touched the very core of the California myth: the founding of Venice Beach, for example, by Abbot Kinney in 1905 was motivated in part by fashionable ideas about eugenics. And, in a very different context, the diagnostic models and sterilization policies developed in California were enthusiastically received by eugenics "researchers" in Europe. The social engineers of Nazi Germany drew directly on the California model. In *Mein Kampf*, Hitler alludes enthusiastically to the eugenics policies implemented in California and, before long, the Nazi symbology of "degenerates" destined for confinement and extermination included the categories of the "Asozial" (the asocial) and the "Arbeitssheu" (the work-shy)—terms reinforced by the eugenics vocabulary of the California experiment. Individuals categorized as "work-shy" wore a black star in Nazi concentration camps.

The pseudo-science behind the earliest camps (at Breitenau, for example, in 1933) can thus be traced, in part, to the teen prisons of the California dream. Replicating its forgotten California affinities, the modern Breitenau facility eventually turned into a reformatory for teenage girls in the 1960s. Ulrike Meinhof, before she went underground as one of the founders of the Red Army Faction, produced a radio documentary in 1969 on the teen inmates of the Breitenau workhouse (which today houses a residence for the mentally ill).

Venice Beach, it turns out, was once the other shore of National Socialism. And the sterilization mill of the Pacific Colony was not far removed from the celebrity enclave of the Malibu Colony: in name and geographical proximity, but also in the disparate fantasies of asylum and experimentation haunting those places.

Youths of all races were confined at the Whittier State School, but the percentage of Chicano and African-American inmates (aged 12 to 17 years) was disproportionate to their numbers in the general population. The range of case files supplying the language of the teen "wards" (and their families) for these poems reflects this imbalance. In addition, the poems capture the eugenics vocabulary used by fieldworkers to condemn and curtail the infidel path of the work-shy, placing this jargon in contact with the direct speech of the inmates.

Text in italics always indicates the voices of the "wards," while text without quotation marks or italics conveys the words of the fieldworkers. Passages in quotes convey the voices of the wards, or of their families and friends, cited indirectly by the fieldworkers. In some case files, all direct statements by teen inmates were deliberately suppressed, producing an absent profile now made visible in these poems.

"Translation" of the lengthy case files required extreme condensation and painstaking assemblage. But the verbal constraint remained in effect throughout the process of writing and revision: the language of these poems derives solely from the case files. The names are real.

4

As partial transcriptions, the poems assembled here can be viewed as experiments in investigative poetics: an approach rooted in the methods of documentary sampling and assemblage—a form of close listening that sustains a history of strong feelings. Originally compiled to justify the elimination of certain populations, the case files can now function—contrary to their original purpose—as a mutable archive of infidel expression, practice, and knowledge.

The ensemble of poems is entitled "Lost Privilege Company"—the name of the isolation unit at the Whittier State School where youthful offenders could be sentenced under harsh conditions for misconduct. Suicides in 1939 and 1940 by two Hispanic teens in solitary confinement brought unprecedented public scrutiny of the prison's history and methods.

TEACUP BUSINESS

cab corny op
  nab crop coy
    ban coop cry
      cab coy porn
        can boy crop
      cab crop yon
    narc bop coy
    narc boy cop
cap boon cry
  racy bop con
    cap born coy
      cap bro cony
        cap boy corn
      cop ya bronc
    cop ya bronc
  cap by croon
crap cob yon
  crap boy con
    crap by coon
      carp boy con
        carp by coon
      car cob pony
    car bony cop
  yarn cob cop
nary cob cop
  nay cob crop
    pray cob con
      pay cob corn
        yap cob corn
      crap cob yon
    racy bop con
  cab coon pry
cop ya bronc

    cop ya bronc!

not a dirtier boy   in the house vile
and effeminate

taking shorts cuts across orchards
    breaking flumes

windows
electric globes

ALEC

            just to hear the noise
                    they make

                        Extra Squad

    a horror of tattling

        stayed for three months
because he *liked the horse*

DIMAS

difficulty in remembering the names of his friends

Mother's Mother's Father

a Cherokee Indian when about
sixty years old *stuck a splinter in his leg
building a gin house.* Blood poisoning de-
veloped and he died shortly afterward.

Bad crowd.

Only disposed to work
under observation.

no "sticktoitiveness"

took about five months
          to get him jiggered up

     third ARrest

     range boy

"Bubbles"
     as he is "dubbed" in the kitchen   a capital dupe
               for the evil-disposed

          the boy's father's wearing
               a bungalow apron

          ¡zefigh!

     someone was looking for me
          someone looking for me

     range boy
     travels with white and black

          says he would *return the money*

          apron motto

such is life
I don't know why

                    no cry-baby   laughs about it
          to think he *couldn't put it over*

13

I might as well be here as any other
            just the place

a little "stand-offish"

                    on one occasion
            allowed carrots and potatoes to burn
she sat by reading

            little brother a "tyrannical bossy street-gamin"

in the habit of *junking*

dances and heap movies

                                FRANCES
                stupid

in the habit of screaming all night

542

eut Feb. 28, 1898.

Figure 1. Bi-racial female, Matilda B (1893). Youth
Authority Records, courtesy of California State Archives,
Office of the Secretary of State, Sacramento.

A mania for stealing bicycles.

Boy's mother had a picture
    taken with her dead triplets
    she very proudly shows to friends.

    Petit larcenist.

Acquainted with picture-show men
who sometimes *give him money*.

    When told to get back into bed said
        "*Oh*, _____" or something similar

fooling along the country road

    near the packing house

CORNELIUS

16

writes obnoxious notes
     to white boys in his company
          all sorts of vile acts   depraved

and this very condition somewhat
   of a "drawing card"   among the boys

   fit subject for an alienist

does show a characteristic towards nomadism
    and a tendency to *get even*

a masturbator.

        JULIUS

     Profane and obscene
   early learned to steal and keep "a cave"
down by the bay   robbed a number
   of glass bottles partly filled with pennies.

        It goes like this   *I heard*
of Jack Johnson   really spoilt
   and made a pet when young

        no place to get it
I crooked it off'n him

had to be taken out of school and strapped frequently

might as well have been a table
                    as a father
        I'd rather get out

            and lose my relatives

Propositus wishes
they had not been   JOSEPHINE

No one ever wanted such a creature
                    always sorry for her *contrary spells*

she does not know her salary
        working at the riveting machine at Levi-Strauss

                    because she would not *dare*
                            open the envelope

Fireman had his *hands burned*, etc
found a small crow-bar to which the goat had been tied
with this crow-bar *Dorito broke the lock*
and Ralph pulled the switch and broke out
the red glass.

The wind blowd out the light.

Propositus
a glutten over suffering   would do mean things and
say he did it *just for fun*

on fire says
Workhouse Detail   D O R I T O

ear candling

shows a lot of spontaneous "drollness"

to all questions

I don't know

mother calls his playthings "junk"

all boys are "alike" to him

JOHN

onset of incorrigibility unknown
but has been "trickish"   since a child

likes to smoke and read the funny papers
a trifling boy
and animal books

a fighty boy

will slap his pals in the face
as soon as the Supervisor's back is turned

what couldn't I do
just as well sitting down   OSCAR

Worn asphalt road, no walks. Kerosene lights. City water.
Three junk dealers within the block.

A good boy requires careful handling.

He would have *the law put on him*

just as soon kill
a man as *have any*

argument with him

worked in candy factory at $4 per week

21

DISCUSSION

Sumary of heredity: (11) Paternal side,-sex immorality; delinquency (Whittier State School), alcoholism and feeble-mindedness. Maternal side,-sex immorality, alcoholism, and feeble-mindedness. Fraternity,-six institutional cases, and three potential delinquents, sex immorality, and feeble-mindedness.

Probable cause of delinquency: (11) Albert's heredity together with his environment are probably the causes for his anti-social conduct.

Social outlook: (11) He will possibly become a permanent institutional case. He should be able to do farm work well if placed in a simple environment. Wherever he is he ought to be able to earn enough to support himself.

Figure 2. Page from eugenics fieldwork report (1921) for Mexican-American male, Albert M, sterilized in 1927. Eugenics Records Office files, courtesy of American Philosophical Society Library, Philadelphia.

Now mama, if I go and do something
            and they come after me,
                        don't you know anything about it.

He had been taught that his mother
had "thrown him away" undertook   E D W A R D

            to cure her ailments by *spiritual methods*

        after her husband killed her father
        she separated from the husband.

Gladys the immoral *colored girl next door*
            gave him talks   on the subject   daily

a cold-blooded schemer
he would undo everything I did

    July 4th he wrote a postal card from Catalina Island
        saying he was *having a vacation*

  the next day
      they found a fifteen page letter
           showing that he had been *studying a code*
               of some sort

if the boy can be reached

      shoe pinched his own foot

Stella Schreiber, cousin, living at 1021 Grand View Ave. Los Angeles

Won't you forgive me for what
    I have done today?

I have never had anyone love me or anyone
                who gave a _____ about me

        you can send me to Lost Privilege Company

FRED   *for saying that word but it is*

            the truth you have wrecked

                    all my wrong tendencies

shows nomadic trait

slept in old barn on pile of straw nights

wants to do everything but
what looks like work

PEDRO

acting as look out for older boys

shows displeasure at correction
by making unnecessary noises

at work

indolent in the extreme

Figure 3. Mexican-American male, Evanisto R
(mirror portrait, 1914), escaped from the Whittier
State School three times in 1915. Youth Authority
Records, courtesy of California State Archives,
Office of the Secretary of State, Sacramento.

When it was suggested that wards were likely to have to drill on saturday
unless they improved Pedro said loudly enough for the whole battalion to hear

Ish gebibble!

PEDRO

removed to Lost Privilege Company

wrote four page letter
to the Superintendent stating that he was *not guilty* that

it could not have been him

apologizes humbly and readily

the old woman poisoned the boy's mind

no man lives that could ever tame me

couldn't remember
two articles if he was sent

to the store

HERBERT

considers himself "pretty wise" he has
silly laughing spells

his chief joy
to collect rubbish and

U R I A H

tear up
American flags *any*
he could get and burn them

oh, I don't know, I just play around

as a method of discipline

the boy's mother *put coal oil on paper   lit it*
and held it to her children's feet

the boy's sister
Mary is a pretty girl
with a nice alto voice but almost too lazy

to use it   *crazy about soldiers and sailors*

is effeminate, a great primper
stands before *the mirror as often* as he can
"giggles like a billy-goat"

would just as leave stab someone

shirks work
whenever possible

deeper than his looks indicate   his babyish

and girlish actions have kept him
from being suspected

works at Fox, Universal, and Alaska Studios
in mob scenes

his former grade-school *teacher*   Mrs.
"feebly inhibited with reference to the lighter and
trivial things in life"
particular fondness

field-worker noticed
many pictures of *Mexican boys in her home*

ERNEST

of the
bestial type

what little mind he has seems to run
in perverted lines

T O N Y

one of the most stupid boys
on the place   defective

should be transferred as soon as possible to Sonoma

the boy's mother would be a good worker
in a moron colony

Is it much further away?

EMILIO

during the interview he told many strange tales

unverifiable and contradictory

a fit candidate for the Pacific Colony

asked if it was a "brain test"

High Grade Moron

my father cried but the judge

the judge would not notice him

I stole a bicycle one night coming home   it was dark
and I was scared
to walk home.

ARTHUR

Awarded the name Peanuts.

Papa is as mean as ever

when he's home you know
how he is don't you

popcorn wagon

HENRY

Henry *give him jiggers*
while the older boy stole
some money

a few times

reported to be neglecting
work   always wants to do

something else

for a long time nothing
was heard of him the history of this family

should not be allowed

to be repeated

ALBERT M

I want to be a bakery.

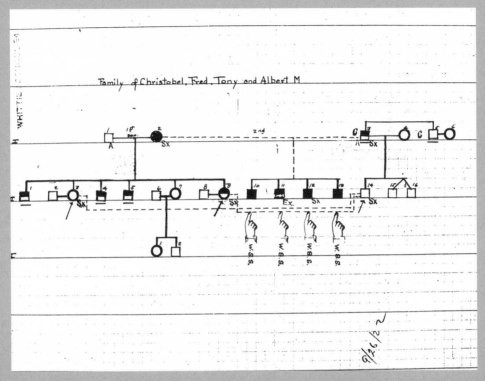

Figure 4. Eugenics genealogical chart for family of Mexican-American male, Albert M (1921). Eugenics Records Office files, courtesy of American Philosophical Society Library, Philadelphia.

We recommend
       his transfer to Sonoma and suggest their machinery
       can furnish more appropriate general supervision.

           Likes to *play marbles*

       thinks a great deal but says little
set fire to a schoolhouse
                     and burned it down

       his eyes would fill with tears
               ("lachrymose excitability")

       it took some time
before the boy's mother (Savaia) could be convinced
                     the visit was a friendly one

       poor comprehension of English   PETE

           stole 200 cigars
                     valued at $20

boy says *it's hard for me to remember*

no pep   *not enough pep*
to move

JOHNNY   needs circumcision

he doesn't *get mad often*
but when he does get mad
he begins to cry.

He found his mother and would *stay*
with her until they found him

under no circumstances
should he be returned to society
to get into more difficulties and eventually procreate
another tainted generation

cannot even erase the board
without resting

not a boy with any close friends

MOTHER
OF PROPOSITUS

"doctor why you don't notify me
befor you perform the operation on him why you

don't ask my consent? I am craz now about my son"

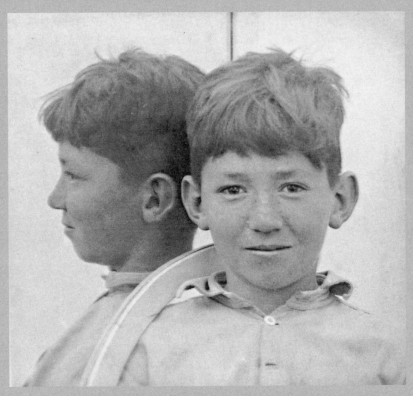

Figure 5. Mexican-American male, Victor R (mirror portrait, 1921). Youth Authority Records, courtesy of California State Archives, Office of the Secretary of State, Sacramento.

"The boy is a puzzle"

turns pale when angry

might go around trying
to kill someone

streetwalker and sniffer of

I told him the truth

picked up
destroying

ALBERTO

electric lights in a tent city

twenty four cuts inflicted with a twisted pocket knife
blade on the head and arms

JACK   *a good deal of this*

sickness   in his   imagination

compelled to move
and broken-hearted   *up north*

don't know what's
become of them
by now

Instructor reports again

"selfish, sensual, secretive, untruthful"

Chief Supervisor says
the boy has been "truthful

and honest
and pretty trustworthy"

refused to talk
and was sent to "thaw out"

sent to Lost Privilege Company
for mauling and kissing another boy   used

to teach younger boys to steal

degenerate
one would almost call him

JESUS

playing bandit

Joe possesses

all the bad characteristics of all the boys

was heard to say

this is the last time
I'm coming in here

twice accused of murder twice acquitted

made a fool of himself
too much already

JOSE

he wanted us to keep on goin' with the bottle

at age 14 went out
to work in the fruit

45

the boy says of himself
I don't get mad easy

a detective found me
took me back again

sleeping at night in a little shack
among the mesquit trees

JAVIER   *working for eats.*

After he'd been "lost track of

for three months"
the boy's mother "mentioned laughingly that he returned home
with some of the money he earned planting onions
still in his pocket"

refused *to go to bed*

declaring he was *not sick*
so that he collapsed all at once

used to *slip off to Venice*

or some other beach

the boys stole cigarettes
from a Japanese store

which they *sold to some tramps.*

Father's second wife killed by some Indian
in the absence of the husband.

A 6 cent car line on the same street.

At Juvenile Hall fairy tales
interest him chiefly

he merely "sits"   J A V I E R

making no attempt
to work

Figure 6. Mexican-American male, Edward Leiva, suicide at age 17 in isolation unit (Lost Privilege Company), mirror portrait showing him in 1935 at age 13. Youth Authority Records, courtesy of California State Archives, Office of the Secretary of State, Sacramento.

Then he turned up suddenly in El Paso, Texas.

Needs taming.

One day he took all the new brooms
              and cut off the handles   then again
              he cut the locks off the lockers—said he wanted them
                    to make something

MAN IS SERIOUSLY CUT

Told to put on his "best clothes"

the judge sent me here

a "boy and a chair" fell over
      but he kept on

        reading

        never "batted an eye" he knew

he ought not to take it but he wanted it so he *carried it off anyway*

49

Highest intelligence quotient ever found

at Whittier State School
"trying to find his windpipe (with a razor)"

sociability neutral

dogged the game if things did not go
to suit him

at one time he *doped apples*

with cayenne pepper
instead of cinnamon

at present has wandered *somewhere north*

from Arizona

NATHANIEL

(The visit to the family home was made
at night, no pictures were obtainable)

I'd get a pie and ditch

I know what 'ud come to me   WILLIAM

      they never found me out though.

A good pal with the boys who would come around
          and whistle for him
         when there was any adventure afoot

     my uncle let us sleep down in the cellar

   on the old blankets he had had
for the bulldogs
 he used to keep down there.

       The boy worked for a Japanese in the market
   tossing empty lettuce crates on a wagon   thus obtaining

  a dollar each morning

with which to buy a meal, he also indulged in the Hippodrome

    don't lock me in
     I'm here

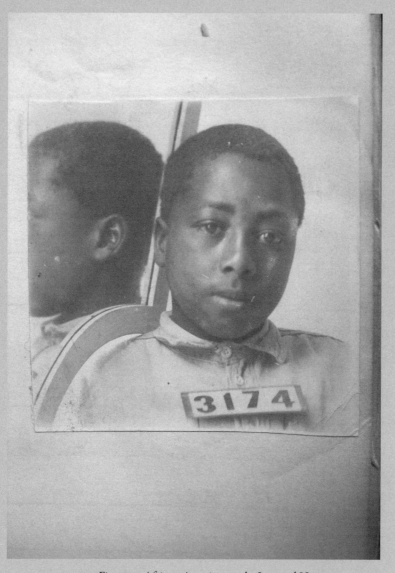

Figure 7. African-American male, Leonard H
(mirror portrait, 1915). Youth Authority Records,
courtesy of California State Archives, Office of the
Secretary of State, Sacramento.

never seemed to progress beyond
the "fairy tale stage"

spent much of his time *at the cave*
the boys had fixed up

with *a table made in sloyd*
an old mattress and an improvised fireplace

Want your buttermilk and ice today?

It will be such a long time
until he is a man that he will forget
in the meantime

if he ever decided
what he wants to do

WILLIAM

his *black cat or his parrot*

"growls" if he isn't allowed to do so

just goes ahead
his own way
keeping the night watchman awake

CARL

questionable company

saved the life of a motion picture actress
giving him some notoriety with *those people*

he was *lonesome and wanted* his bicycle

broke up housekeeping
sings in "minstrels"

the boy's father chose to destroy his wife's clothes
because she is so obviously *fond*
of pretty clothes

never anything but a man

But I was square

and they wouldn't let me go to my little sister's
they used to punish me by not letting me see her

and I hated that most of all.

We all know no good
comes of that mixture.

RAYMOND

To put him in

Lost Privilege Company for 40 days
disobedience
bad talk and disinclination to work

would you ask a fellow to wash the dishes at noon hour?
and would you keep throwing it up to a fellow

after you'd given him a good licking?

Father slanders the boy's dead mother in his presence
is reported
to have beaten the boy on head and body
until he was forced "to scream for help"

plays the cornet

whenever work was to be handed in
his was always strangely
"lost strayed or stolen"

55

reads the dictionary and Mother Goose

> *tore the bed clothes*
>> and everything else he could lay his hands on
>>> *just for meanness*

declared the *bad man had* him

and that was the reason
he *cut up like* he did.

One day he ate *25 cents worth of walnuts*
and *fell into a fever*

JOSEPH

they taught him to steal fruit from wagons

among the things stolen
a hammer a chain and a dog

calls his step-mother "Hazel"

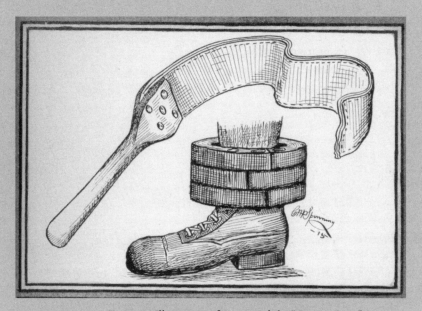

Figure 8. Illustration of a strap and the "Oregon Boot"
used on escapees from the Whittier School (1915). Youth
Authority Records, courtesy of California State Archives,
Office of the Secretary of State, Sacramento.

is observed
to have an enormous appetite
a great big over-sexed boy
keeping late

THEODORE   and unusual hours.

"Mr. Young asked to be allowed
to take him into Mexico as a cook
flunky and servant for himself
and a party of men"

sent
to Lost Privilege Company for refusing to work

breaking dishes maliciously   *throwing peach pits*
making improper insinuations

about a small boy

He declared "she wanted to leave home
just like other girls do

and I was glad to have her go"

disagreeable *back of the church*.

    (Night call arranged
    to see the father personally)

use of the "Oregon Boot"
    to inhibit runaways.

            H E L E N

    Tendency to take the world
        as a joke   unable to keep her

    a minute after supper

THE BOOK
OF LISTENING

Listening and being voiceless often go hand in hand, but could *speech* become a way of listening?

To listen without fault, one must have permission to listen. This forgotten truth about listening reveals itself in the distinctions between listening, overhearing, and eavesdropping. Without permission—outside an unmarked circle of intended listeners—one might accidentally overhear a phrase, perhaps to the detriment of oneself and others. But this helpless circumstance also resembles an incident of listening under compulsion, of *hearing voices*. Even further from the speaker's consent, one may deliberately conceal oneself in the shadows of eavesdropping.

The poem hovers between the obligation to seek permission to listen and the impossibility of obtaining it from a voice that cannot be reached.

How does one go about seeking permission to listen to voices that have never been heard—or never existed? By reckoning and sacrifice? Or by solicitation and prayer?

Perhaps we could sound the lost words of others by using a device made of words. Not a prayer exactly, but a divining tool: a teacup floating across a ouija board, a toy summoning a "translation" from the other side. A cliché tumbled until it yields a conversation, a riddle. A little teacup business.

Seeking permission to listen begins by acknowledging the submerged will or disposition of voices that have been silenced. We might presume that a lost voice would welcome the chance to be heard, but this presumption ignores the need to ask for consent. It is always possible that the unknown voice may insist on *remaining silent*. It may *refuse* permission.

Must the words we solicit always be loan words—not owned or possessed for good—as Sappho acknowledges in her prayer to Aphrodite, asking to borrow the words of a spell to bewitch her lover?

The project of listening, or seeking permission to listen, might not be merely the first step in a process that leads to a more active stance of writing or composing. The fate of the listener, or the gesture seeking permission to listen, may be preserved in a speech act, so that writing proceeds without possessing a voice.

Having somehow gained permission to listen to an unknown voice, must one pledge not to harm or betray that voice? What would that mean? And would it ever be possible *not* to break one's vow, one's oath, to the voices one has solicited?

What exactly do we hope to discover by listening to voices that have been lost or silenced? History, images, music? Unfamiliar ways of thinking and speaking? Perhaps we listen for emotional cues or triggers, which may cause one to turn away, or to act without thinking—to fulfill a pact to which one is inscrutably bound. Could we say that we sometimes listen for *relic feelings*? And in that moment of attention, could we be listening to detect traces of *bare life*, conceived as the ground of collectivity?

Again, we must ask: can speech that performs the act of listening—a poem seeking permission to listen—satisfy an aversion to theatricality, to drawing attention to oneself? Perhaps the ethics of close listening can only be fulfilled by speaking to no one—to oneself—as a circuit, a procedure, for hearing voices.

CREEDMOORBLANCA

From the "orphan asylums" of California, we seek to occupy other sites where dialects of the broken and furious language of confinement may be found: the Psychiatric Clinic in Heidelberg, Germany (home of the legendary Prinzhorn Collection), a repository of art and writings of the insane confiscated by the Nazis in 1933; the Breitenau Workhouse, turned into a Concentration Camp (also in 1933), its first prisoners an assortment of drifters and runaways, idlers and troublemakers, beggars and daydreamers, culled from the streets. We also remember the New York State Training School for Girls, where the fifteen-year-old Ella Fitzgerald was confined in 1933 and marked as "ungovernable" (a prelude to sterilization) before she escaped and went on to fulfill her musical destiny. We return to the Farm Colony of the Brooklyn State Hospital, founded in 1912 and later to become the vast Creedmoor Psychiatric Center, where a teenage Lou Reed underwent electroshock "therapy" in 1959, and where the revelation of beatings and the death of a disturbed inmate in the Secure Unit brought public scrutiny in 1983.

On this path, we find it impossible to leave behind the shadowy test-subjects of the Pacific Colony for the Feebleminded, to escape the kids who were tagged as misfits, morons, delinquents, perverts, imbeciles, and outcasts. We discover their institutional fate, and the vocabulary used to sort them into grades of incorrigibility, in other dark places. The apparatus built to make fugitive lives disappear extends to the isolation and disposal of the insane.

In taxonomies of social deviance, mental illness is a category of subnormality distinct from delinquency, feeblemindedness, or degeneracy. Yet the procedures and nomenclatures binding these apparently disparate populations are intertwined. The ideological equation of the deranged and the delinquent discloses the overlapping social fate of these two modes of waywardness. The sterilization mills of California were as likely to neuter the lunatic as the derelict. And in Nazi Germany in 1937, artifacts produced by the insane (drawn from the Prinzhorn Collection) were displayed alongside examples of "degenerate art."

Seizing upon the dialectical surplus of this equation, one discovers that the writings of the insane, which sometimes call to mind episodes of "speaking in tongues," testify with perfect clarity and specificity to the aggravating deprivations of confinement, the generosity of worklessness, and the disposition of revolt. From this perspective, the gibberish crafted by the insane harbors, as one might expect, fiery complaints but also lucid testimony: a medium of countersigns akin to the infidel speech found in "Lost Privilege Company."

In youth prisons and locked asylums for the chronically insane, "Confinement," as Avery Gordon and Ines Schaber assert in their investigation of the Breitenau Workhouse, "is a means by which unwanted people, threatening ideas, and impermissible fellowships are outlawed and made invisible, inaccessible, illegible, and illegitimate." At the same time, an archive that once served the ends of repression "confines or encloses the very ideas it is designed to silence or make invisible"; it preserves "documents of a fugitive knowledge"—a record of incarceration that also yields a garbled treasury of infidel culture. The evidence of confinement is thus haunted by testimony directed towards history in presentiments, in flash-forward—by wishes as yet unfulfilled. And this fugitive knowledge contains "a feeling for justice."

Expanding what the poet Susan Howe calls "the telepathy of the archive," the poems of *The Work-Shy* contain "a deposit of a future yet to come." To say that a record of confinement may harbor an intimation of justice or hope implies that the documentary shadow it casts is also pointing ahead, undischarged, premonitory—one of the peculiar hiding places of anticipatory consciousness. Ernst Bloch's conception of the "ontology of *not-yet-being*" helps to revise our sense of the potentiality of language, deeds, and daydreams that have not achieved full expression in the past but now point towards a still unrealized future: a utopian surplus. *Nothing happens only in the time in which it first appeared*, Gordon and Schaber explain.

In our investigations, we are also trying to account for the halting movement from "transcription" to a way of making poems that veers towards charlatanism and fraud, towards the teacup business of the ouija board—towards the "we-position" of translation. Yet when translation circles from English to English (from base texts that have sometimes already been translated from German or French), what exactly are we doing? Could we say that we are listening—closely, actively—to internees, inmates, to those who have been "turned in" for their actions or beliefs, to those on the inside?

Yes, we are listening, and seeking permission to listen, under a powerful constraint: these poems (unlike those of "Lost Privilege Company") render solely the voices of inmates, apart from the killing language of the overseers. We are listening to the inside of the outside. "We are practicing the art of talking about what we have not yet experienced," Gordon and Schaber affirm.

It may be useful to call these translations "variants" or "variations" of the base texts—writings by inmates of American and European asylums between 1909 and 1980—of which the originals were written mostly in prose, varying in length from two to ten pages. As in the case of the "Lost Privilege Company" poems, "turning" the base text called for steep compression and careful assemblage—the craft of *détournement*—grafting samples to form a chain of ragged soliloquies, kenning and keening, riddles and rants. But the basic verbal constraint is unyielding: every word of these poems is borrowed or begged from obstinate texts, from the writings of individuals held in asylum. The names are real.

These highly condensed variants could also be called *versions,* since they convert the base text (usually prose) into verse—another kind of constraint: winnowing, built, broken, controversial. Following intuitions shared by documentary and lyric poetries, the versions presented here retain the typographical anomalies of the base texts: misspelling, faulty grammar or syntax, underlining, use of capital letters, and so on. Despite such eccentricities, the original texts were not usually conceived as art by their authors; they were diary entries, treatises, tabulations, prayers, rants, testimonials, letters undelivered. They are witness to asylum.

As variants, these poems "translate" the base texts out of the discourse of solipsistic madness (a framework that isolates the lunatic—in most peoples' minds—from society) into a wider field of social conflicts and correspondences. We "turn" the base texts away from madness in order to reveal how the writings of the insane document the social conditions of confinement, the unrest of idleness, and wishful thinking about a better life. As "concise ornaments of utopian substance," these translations crystallize feelings and thoughts found in the base texts, which could rightly be mistaken for the scribbling of the unsettled, of misfits, wanderers, and blasphemers.

CREEDMOORBLANCA, the title of this group of poems, is a word coined by Samuela Joy Blank, who was an African-American inmate at the Creedmoor Psychiatric Center.

Base Translation
Roger Cardinal
Sophie Hawkes
Sarah and Peter B. Hoffman
Claudia Stoeffler
Kiko Gaskell and Peter Jones

TEACUP BUSINESS

cab corny op
  ban coop cry
    pray cob con
      cab coy porn
        con a bop cry
      nab crop coy
    narc boy cop
    narc bop coy
cap boon cry
  racy bop con
    cap born coy
      cap bro cony
        crap cob yon
      crap boy con
    cop coy barn
  bar cony cop
carp boy con
  car bony cop
    yarn cob cop
      nary cob cop
        nay cob crop
      pray cob con
    yap cob corn
  cob con a pry
con a bop cry
  bra cony cop
    cop con bray
      bay con crop
        bay corn cop
      racy bop con
    cab coon pry
  cab corny op
con a bop cry

    con a bop cry!

CARBON COPY

83

One screams *clik* and the other *cluk*,
the policeman standing there

sends greetings should you
need draft horses

you can have them,
pencil on paper, undated.

And vows death.
No visiting privileges

for time and eternity
should serve as a warning to you

in the best fashion of deception.
Sworn in,

pivots between two birds
my plan to release myself.

ALOIS

the delinquent's seemliness
ordering and confirming thus

the rule of internal order
hiccupping at the heavy

bottom of a very recent penetrating test
the still deliquescing but repentant

delinquent daydreaming
crying fearfully but cheerfully for nothing

thinking of the poor
fool of the accident

MARMOR

miscreants
and other debonair

bad men the sow says in a bubble
LEAVE ME

I'LL GET OUT OF IT ALONE

BARBARA

Not real—she said
never real, alarm

spreads, locked in people
everywhere testing

and labeling each other
using hand signals and a plague

of rhyming words—
this massive public secret

THEODOR

Oh, please
forgive
I have written
Theodor
with a pencil
it was done
in a case of emergency

Almost seventeen months
it's been since I was confined
to your intelligence
in common with my fellow internees
only the effluvia of your gaze.

What goes on in this place of caring, rest
and tranquility the most hateful
establishment for incarceration
on the spot investigations
but an atom of

what goes on
amid the universal masses
my file comprising
over a thousand pages
even adding weight to the direction

in which a being might incline
to undergo an interrogation
we internees are all subject
to hyperexcitation
we are a special breed.

The new situation

SYLVAIN

taking shape in the wings
without spilling a single drop
hoodwinked for centuries
our bellyful of being locked up this is
your once and final warning

Kgl. Heilanstalt Weinsberg.   Speise-3

	Sonntag 12.	Montag 13.	Dienstag 14.
1. Klasse Mittagessen	Grünkernsuppe Ochsenmaulsalat Roastbraten Bohnen, Salzkartrf. Eiermilch mit Bisquitt.	Nudelsuppe Siedfleisch Gelberüben Königsberger Klösse Salzkartoffeln. Dampfäpfel.	Sagosuppe Zwiebelpastetchen Schupfnudeln Kohlräbchen Auflauf.
2. Klasse Mittagessen	Grünkernsuppe Roastbraten eing.Bohnen,Salzkart. Eiermilch mit Bisquitt.	Nudelsuppe Königsberger Klösse Salzkartoffeln. Dampfäpfel.	Sagosuppe Schupfnudeln Bodenkohlraben. Auflauf.
1. Klasse Abendessen	Tee. Braten i.Eiertunke Butter,Schalenkartoffeln.(statt Brot)	Tee. Ged. Herz Kartoffelbrei.	Tee. Eierkuchen Salat.
2. Klasse Abendessen	Tee. Kalten Braten,Butter Schalenkartoffeln (statt Brot.)	Tee. Schinkenwurst Kartoffelbrei.	Tee. Eierkäs,Salat.
3. Klasse Mittagessen a	Sagosuppe Siedfleisch Bodenkohlraben.	Kartoffelsuppe Siedfleisch Zwiebeltunke,Kart.	Gerstensuppe Sauerkraut ger.Kartoffeln.
Mittagessen b	Kohlraben mit Fleisch.	Saure Kartoffeln mit Fleisch.	Kartoffelbrei mit Fleisch.
3. Klasse Abendessen a	Riebelensuppe Preswurst,Kartoffeln.	Selleriesuppe Käse,Kartoffeln.	Gerstensuppe ger.Fleisch,P.Gurken.
Abendessen b	Milchnudeln.	Milchbrei.	Sagobrei.

Figure 9. Ink writing on institutional meal plan
(1915), August Klett. Copyright Prinzhorn Collection.
University Hospital Heidelberg. Inventory no. 533.

Frog stare

Rider stare

Clamp stare

Staff stare, 21 times

In-the-lead stare (always view slits, holes, things left below)

Assessing stare

Whale stare

10er stare (look at 10 nice things for a long time)

HYACINTH

Me, I adore my beauty shop equipment.
It's there that the worst crimes
take place and when they rebelled
with me they set off
they saw flames et cetera in the thing
but it can't
badly it's done
by specialists I know very well
it can't hurt anybody
I did nothing wrong to them.

To attack indirectly because they see
I don't know how to speak,
their nerves shot those who are calm
to hear the tables of voices
[from here on Jacqueline sobs until the end]
aside from my business
it's the most beautiful day of my life
why must I give things
I don't have
to others oh mama said this and then me.

at the lever of the grinding ornament
vexations of the state's flashiness
pale brat chills

the wrong oath in its
word—tickle and burn—
the foliage oven of the rope's decay

eyes fixed to the ground there
are still prisoners coming
something lasting

and durable in plant shade

AUGUST

swallows like a goose that's just eaten
goldfish-corn and suddenly cackles
all languages at once in rabbit *quack quack*

the morning of the pupil's blue life

the ray-stung aft-eye
with which
I don't want to give you a well as a present

who owns a lampwhip of the gold of gasolinechalk
a dish of lentils in the hands of slumber
the winged bottlery

Figure 10. Hand-embroidered asylum jacket of Agnes Richter (made between 1890 and 1900). Copyright Prinzhorn Collection. University Hospital Heidelberg. Inventory no. 743.

my jacket is

me

my jacket is

I am not

I am not going home

AGNES R

55th DAY OF MY SOLITARY CONFINEMENT

memory of my stay in a Rest Home
the real disciples unaware of themselves
like everybody else

with whom ardent ex-sunset
in time alas! and bitterly farrowing
not knowing the "meanwhile" to his detriment

the only one worthy of the name
a fool for whom "no" spins off the rattled
unknown and viperous language

—that way it about-ships itself
clairvoyant sore peep all
rite now in the fur row

MARMOR

split-sleeping in the Wind that worries its
creamature and creamating
for work that's "e-z to wax"

Just try to pretend nothing is going on.
With that in mind you notice
like you do every once in a while
the sprinkler above the desk.

You just stare into that metal god.
The door is closed so no one sees
("system inmate" for twelve years)
the sun setting over the stone city.

BETH

I have not been in the

I am not so

AGNES R

And when we rebelled
of course you had what they called

an hearing I don't remember any
night-worker giving out stuff.

She also did my hair

the radio going & people
waking you up for cigarettes

(I don't smoke) going
through your drawers

looking for clothes to steal
people downstairs in lock up

feeling it was their right
to come upstairs

KAROSELLE

and ask stupid questions
so everybody wasn't all thrown together

and people couldn't pick fights
weren't together. No, when you reffuse

to get up in the morning
all the white people getting ready.

I wont tangle with polly ticks gobbleup
like gadflies on parade
millet airy march parts leave that bee

under ground wan the ghoul
closes its eyes to natter,
closes its gob, those animals

opening their cowl are forced
to shut up those birdles
those worn out poisons, Joker

Scoff right youthicky
canter Burr Hive guzzled all the
hooch getcha hands off theirs

AIMABLE

HYACINTH

To walk is somewhat more abstract than life.

Take the idea of the soul in nature
—though man can hardly intrude into nature.

To counteract airplane sickness
I somersault to the east on a blue sofa.

Lively contemplation of the science of the will.

We view in advance the nervous element
of the following parts as gifted with will:

right toenails & right knee (both whole),
hip, teeth (clenching), beard,
right eye, female thought of the male,
backwards edge of the head.

Tiny gas bubbles wherever
can surely be looked at societologically.

The forgotten is not defenseless!

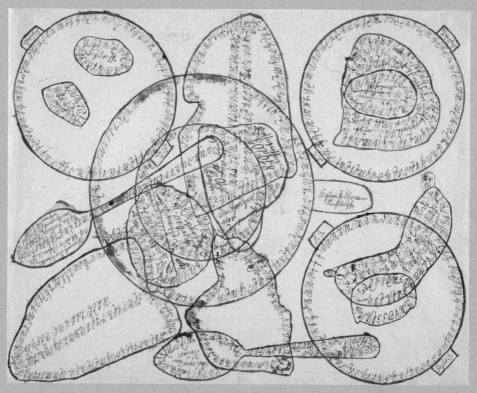

Figure 11. Ink and pencil text/drawing (1910), Barbara Suckfüll. Copyright Prinzhorn Collection. University Hospital Heidelberg. Inventory no. 1960.

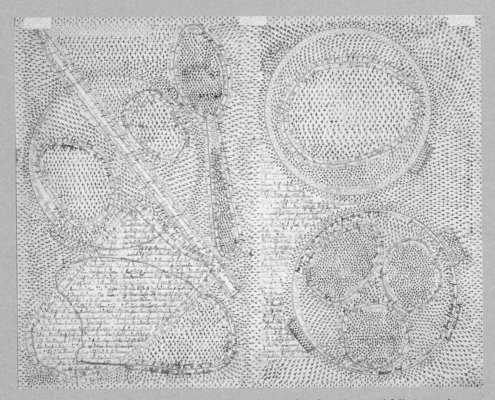

Figure 12. Ink and pencil text/drawing (1910), Barbara Suckfüll. Copyright Prinzhorn Collection. University Hospital Heidelberg. Inventory no. 1957.

Puppets are so tiny
Bordello curoweight
with novelty pancakes

Ore below the fishmarkets is the fish-
pond gotha cup the
market Charon

AIMABLE

OUTSIDE

The Outcast: _____

The Poet (as she moves closer from a distance):

The Outcast: In the end there is

The Poet: _____

The Telephone, Gliding Past: That's the way it is!

The Outcast: It pleases fate
           to put in a word.

The Telephone: _____

The Outcast: Because that which is near
             only grants a delay of the shadow of fate.
             The uncertain does not fit into everything.

The Poet: But if the nearby is the world
          the poet disappears
          comet-like into
          clouds of others.

The Outcast: I grant the Telephone the fact.

The Poet: The fact counts on the Doing,
          the Telephone puts in the word.

          Fantasy is the most silent of realities.

Lord of the Cloister: The comet comes with prayer
                and disappears with it *yes-yes*
                the thing itself
                the thing often is the "no"

Local Lady: Everybody serves the Lady member of an order.

Lady in Blue: Said Lady is privy to the life dreams of world reason.

Lady in Red: Those farthest away from home draw nearer to each other.

Local Lady: That strangeness from the Men's World
                indicates the non-virtue of overrating.

The Outcast: Give hints to the tender.

The Poet: Like night rain on the site of the apparition.

INSTRUCTIONS

The Ladies' World itself, along with other worlds demonstrated here, moves outside the sequence of phenomena if the rectangular point of view and manner of speaking impart a significance in which they necessarily rearrange themselves for reality in some larger societal form.

The Poet who appears here actually interprets it that way until he spots the Outcast seeing in him the final representation of his poetry, which now stirs up sympathy for a time—like any poetry, Telephone, and passion in their new formulation. And it is similar with sentence formation.

AGNES R

brother freedom

tiny cherries

He hears no voices.
He hears a voice.
He hears no voices.
He hears a voice.
He hears no voices.
He hears a voice.

KARL

Oh Karly!
you are going to be locked up.

I have no particular thing to occupy me.

I know things,
I know that I know them,
and I know that I know that I know them.

I cry out after some known-unknown Thing
as I hurry over my sand and barrenness. Oh,
Kind Devil, if you are not to fetch me Happiness

then slip from your great steel key-ring
a bright little key to the door of the glittering
bad things and give it to me.

MARY M

dear god cried Marguerite
thud ore is of eye ron
it can nobby oh penned
the poor wee thing
at this very mow meant
once the Forwards are in control
the Backs are there ready
to back up any break throughs.

Resolute in dummies and feints

the knew waves soldered for currents
it's an active resource
hard to short-circuit you bring
down accidents and fires
it is ness ess-
erry for the acids
to be adjusted
to the accumes.

Take your hat off
you dare ask my par don
and tell me why you winter way,
peck sailor
you'll get the orange
deduced therefrom
the perfect science of the scalpel
at eight o'clock midnight

SYLVAIN

YOU ARE SOMEBODY

SANDIE

one must do this one must
do that it's rebellion a little it's fine
to see rebellion et cetera it happens
all the time but the secret police

like you I don't know how to answer
the secret police
also to prove that the makalam of promakalam
prokalastarrokalarembrokelastrrmakalastostemarlokerster

he said that good girls are good
like you but the rules don't allow it
before someone, oarsman,
who has never been to school

who has not done this
when you talk like that all alone
you don't know how to say it
you must scream through everything

you see them you always see them rebel he says
thas why thas why they possess
the gift of language
I think it's the blow

I think it's the blow
the man downstairs
gave me on the forehead
it's not like I saw black

but like a bar that possessed the gift
of languages he said repeat after me, me
I look around like anybody else
I don't look into the eyes of someone

when one is a little too close to explain
oneself in that room nevertheless
I hate them since what's been done to me
he says because you rebel the house will be

the same he says if I sit down he says
you should rebel to be fashionable.

When I look parallel with a candle
I am God for each man kills
the thing he loves, stolen F.B.I.
bicycle, incredible speed, black boy
and it's thought to be incarcerated filth,
as one outsider might say
to another, steal
a philodendron leaf.
Full of locks and keys and tunnels.

No person, no death.
And I being poor
have only my dreams,
essence of winter's lust.
Hooked on platitudes.
The low relevancy twist isn't

enough to incarcerate
a 300-lb. sodden mass
but get it stripped down
it comes easy.
An equation adding up to
NO RETURN.

The big C sets in—
afraid? me?
Ain't gonna be no auxiliary cop,
hit a candle parallel
and you got God he's
due around 11 p.m.

Stigmatized by habeas corpus,
miracle of the shoe slip-sole
insert of the ruthlessly sacrificed
declared-as-dead victim, her hair

wound into this four-page idiomatic
picture pinned up with combs
demanding revenge—
"hair for a hair"

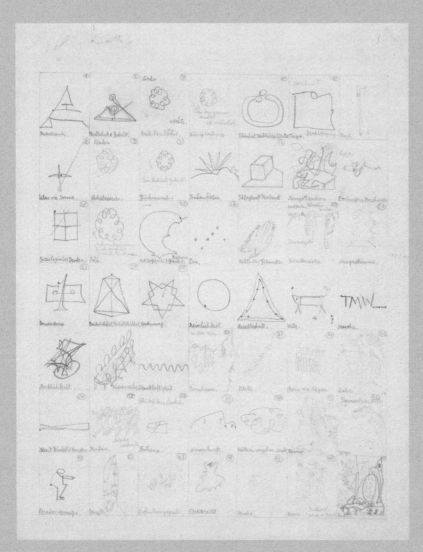

Figure 13. Pencil text and drawing (date unknown),
Hyacinth Freiherr von Wieser. Copyright Prinzhorn
Collection. University Hospital Heidelberg. Inventory no.
2438.

One nee on the ground.
The nees placed on the Plinth.
Nees tensed but not locked.
The nees in three-quarter view.

Words thick.

Right forearm posed upright,
almost perpendicular,
the Plinth,
the words white petticoat.

All indispensable means.
Quiet person of medium height
locked up for no good reason.
Flag as hinge, collar, frame—

master face half extinguished.

EMILE

Seedy bra hymn
Car fishtailing
Dawn Pencil X 1000-2
Halfweigh
Tutch-tastic

Neath the vorts of heaven
Theirl be Happy nessin
The faithless night
Tick science bimbam
Red lipstick great stuff

Your hole randsome of mizz airy.

SYLVAIN

where to prod
exactly on the tender foreknowledge
wonderings whamming
whose owllike smuttings
the re-
capitulation, night's capricious giving in
to the throne, dementia
whooze heir
looms the size of pinpoints
doubled by doldrums
(fishy and dunmarked) deeded rightly
and practiced nightly until this
deeped in seeping
sac of hair and doom
while, as the obligatory ½
pleasure swells fullblown in destiny,
crouching ready inme kin
of sodden saints worth but sick damns
spoonfed ways an offscene
stab in darkness
the scrambly fixings
of one's mother obeying the obstructions.

tit city councilor
of war to my bosses
who have me in prison
many years already

murder asylum!!!

the horrible ladles and forks
what have I seen
demand release
my son demand from this

murderer's hut

Due to urgent necessity of purely thinking
and affirmative matter
THE ALPHABETIC CHARACTER
as against
THE PERSON IN SILENCE
am forced to ask here
in the interest of all science everywhere
most politely
whether I may take
one sheet of writing paper
and one envelope of my choice
from the stock of writing materials.

So far as these permissions
sought in this matter
by means of these
LINES OF WRITING
may be granted
due to the need for something
singular I also request most kindly
at the same time
the return of this sheet of PAPER,
specially technically
prepared by _____
and permitted to be handed such.

The corresponding <u>NOTE OF APPROVAL</u> is requested <u>HEREUNDER</u>.

<u>IN NOTHING</u> read,

Hermit unassuming
I do not want to run away!

Because I can demand that I be
released I want to wait for that.

To fulfill the custom
to replace one idea

with another
—and that is a struggle!

Who is it gathers in the apples?
Who is it makes great tipple?

What merit has the man who devours?
Where is the potter red potter?

What is an arsenal?

What does I've had my furglow mean?
What does I've had my furlough mean?

Little kids girls boys watch out
before you go leaping over brooks.

Why do we sing I must away?
What might happen if this is the case?

What is meant by a cliff?

What makes us start singing
wenwee step on the cowplanks?

Which is more intelligent the dresser
or the one who needs his wounds dressed?

What is meant by the word insects?
What is a packet of bandages?

Where is the governor of the prison?

What is his name?

Neither tipple nor trout.

AIMABLE

Figure 14. Pencil text (1910), Valentin Franz Maier.
Copyright Prinzhorn Collection. University Hospital Heidelberg.
Inventory no. 3631.

I saw you blush
like a cup of Ship
in the auto-orchid,
in the arms of
the general headquarters
on its knees, whither
goest thou lord,
ouchy bouquet,
ouchy often free of charge
in music little Geisha chrysanthemum
[the red Catherine on horseback]
naked in the cords of
the sphinx of the [...] painted inside

Volunteer one year
Communard
One day as day-boy
Watched how

To incise, to mill,
To soak, to rotate,
To heat up
The holders crammed with letters.

Molded in wax on slate, a bee
With its garter, a tiny saint's
Medallion, the saddle, 2 mannikins,
The light turned up.

Glossary of Undertitles.
Counted out the bed linen,
Set out the bed linen,
Made his bed.

Changed the bed linen, took a train,
Shook out his curtains.
Writings as Boarder.
Dictation. Stories. Logical

Analysis. Natural History. Grammar.
The Ten Parts of Speech
Describe his workshop.
Describe his incarceration.

EMILE

unless <u>taken away from here</u>
        <u>by tonight</u>

        will until to-

    morrow   E R W I N

stare at the sun
or bash in <u>my temple</u> with a post

JULES

My code Whorizons larst yere
awl those carves the cold woz in Tents
when eyewash in daws
the souls of mye pheet
wurr perry shin soak tins punk.

Mye bruthiz cunt tay kit
I've brung mye cell foff
timon timon gayne.
that swye the prossy cuter
reely hazzit infamee.

JULES

Mye purr purse in right ing Ister
tellyew a thinger too bean ayble to stay putt
aint summink the lyksa yew kandoo

Ive lost tutch with mye selph
Ide bee blyged iff yoo
cood spair a pockit hanker cheef for Jools

Tooby plucky saye Hang
onn Eye cood Boase toff havin skraipt
throo bye the skinner mye teath

mye syst her througher alms
surround mye nekk Yore syst
hearse herb itch Getcher sell foam

JULES

Ellsyle Screem fore help.

Migh pokkit adder nole innit
sew the butta nopen dupp
it woz Perry Shin Coal
and mye danda juss droopt.

Mizz triss Owe shuns sheap sheap
mye poop eel aint lye kew.
The woodz cum rite down inter the orch idza
long the paive meant.

Eye wenter the howse ter sea
ware the figher woz Ide herd sum won crigh nowt
figher mye alms broak mye lex herd
doan choo shout noh lowder

else aisle lok yupp.

JULES

Jen tall men Imer batchel ler

wen Eye git Ohm
ittlebee boy lingott
Ime loo zing bludd Inn ear
dayday daybyday

JULES

Figure 15. Pencil text (1909), Emma Hauck, letter to her husband. Copyright Prinzhorn Collection. University Hospital Heidelberg. Inventory no. 3621.

Our words are like people.

We talk and react to words
like crowds in the streets

PAUL

as they look up at the big lightbulb
clock, the six changing to seven, the seven

rapidly adding a curved bottom
and a rounded top

to become eight.
This is the destruction of time.

They are like that
for an idea it's a
fashion of their own their war secret's
not written they hide it
a sorcerer's gun of wood
make no mistake.

Those who could be called
top or robot
they have that precision
in their soul it's their own
idea for sure
make no mistake.

HENRI

JULIUS

asylum Oh you

sad word

And I want privacy so much
but then some clock keeps saying

I can't be left alone.
What if no one ever comes

here to get me?
I'll try to find someone

to kill me, if you know
maybe you can take me

by surprise. And my gosh!
isn't it always a surprise

That goes for the smallest
to the biggest, object
or non-object.

Omnipotence-moths, et cetera,
et cetera, always quite comfortable
riding information

ADOLF

but I booze a whole stable bucket,
full it must be, and lock myself in the chamber.
That way the fairy-like side bay

of aforesaid wood gully
at the entrance of which aforesaid
Trikadero does what it says.

False complaints
about unrest

and refusal to work now
they are taking us with force.

Many have asked for me
but all are refused meetings

with me not even animals
wait that long, even animals cry

if they are separated
that long for this reason they

put me together upstairs
with the prisoners

LORENZ

container empties out and gets
refilled with simple effort
but liquid has to be fetched

from the source the latter is near
at hand the former
a long way off

The early hour hath gold in its mouth.

Exactology.

Write books for 3 hours,
outside if possible.

Practice poses,
don't reach across to the other side.

No magic seeing.

Predict occult with pencil.
Sleep for 1 second.

Don't look at the bottom of the spoon.

Night handwashing.
Jump into bed. Roll up inside
blanket from the northwest.
Boldly fall asleep (80 ways).

       Sirius. Don't touch
       prick. Calculate.

       No star love.

Asyl

I today women

AGNES R

my jacket

my walking

inmate 583

143

I'll be both.
Like the horse in its stall

calling the pheasants home to roost
though they twirl

like burnt bread in a toaster.
As if the night-time glare

of locked doors
could reduce the effect.

JOSEPH

Figure 16. Photograph of Emma Hauck,
mirror portrait (ca. 1909). Copyright Prinzhorn
Collection. University Hospital Heidelberg.

come sweetheart sweetheart come come come sweetheart come
come sweetheart sweetheart come come come sweetheart come
come sweetheart sweetheart   come come come sweetheart come
come sweetheart sweetheart   come come come sweetheart come
come sweetheart sweetheart   come come come sweetheart come
come sweetheart sweetheart   come come come sweetheart come
come sweetheart sweetheart   come come come sweetheart come
come sweetheart sweetheart   come come comesweetheart come
come sweetheart sweetheart   come come comesweetheart come
come sweetheart sweetheart   come come comesweetheartcome
come sweetheart sweetheart   come come comesweetheartcome
come sweetheart sweetheart   come comecomesweetheartcome
come sweetheart sweetheart   come comecomesweetheartcome
come sweetheart sweetheart   comecomecomesweetheartcome
come sweetheart sweetheart   comecomecomesweetheartcome
come sweetheart sweetheart   come comecomesweetheartcome
come sweetheart sweetheart   come comecomesweetheart come
come sweetheart sweetheart   come comecome sweetheart come
come sweetheart sweetheart   come come come sweetheart come
come sweetheart sweetheart   come come come sweetheart come
come sweetheart sweetheart   come come come sweetheart come
come sweetheart sweetheart   come comecome sweetheart come
come sweetheart sweetheart   come comecome sweetheart come
come sweetheart sweetheart   come come come sweetheart come
come sweetheart sweetheart   come come come   sweetheart come
come sweetheart sweetheart   come come come   sweetheart come
come sweetheart sweetheart   come come come   sweetheart come
come sweetheart sweetheart   come come come   sweetheart come
come sweetheart sweetheart   come come come   sweetheart come
come sweetheart sweetheart   come come come sweetheart come
come sweetheart sweetheart   come come come sweetheart come
come sweetheart sweetheart   comecome come sweetheart come
come sweetheart sweetheart   comecome come sweetheart come
come sweetheart sweetheart   comecomecome sweetheartcome
come sweetheart sweetheartcomecome comesweetheartcome

SOURCES

Permission to adapt and reprint texts and archival materials has been kindly granted by the following publishers and institutions:

John G. H. Oakes, publisher and editor (with Donald Kennison). *In the Realms of the Unreal: "Insane Writings."* New York: Four Walls Eight Windows, 1991. With particular obligations and gratitude to the multiple translators of texts in this volume.

American Philosophical Society Library (Philadelphia, PA). Archives of the Eugenics Records Office, fieldworker case files (with the assistance of Charles Greifenstein). Special thanks to Miroslava Chavez-Garcia.

California State Archives, Fred C. Nelles School for Boys (Whittier) records, Office of the Secretary of State, Sacramento, California. Special thanks to Miroslava Chavez-Garcia.

Prinzhorn Collection, Center for Psychosocial Medicine, University Hospital (Heidelberg, Germany). Special thanks to Sabine Hohnholz, Curator and Archivist of the Sammlung Prinzhorn.

In addition, *The Work-Shy* has been shaped by the scholarly, theoretical, and editorial labors of the following collaborators:

Miroslava Chavez-Garcia. *States of Delinquency: Race and Science in the Making of California's Juvenile Justice System*. Berkeley: University of California Press, 2012.

Ines Schaber and Avery F. Gordon. *The Workhouse (Breitenau Room) / Das Arbeitshaus (Raum Breitenau)*. Köln: Verlag der Buchhandlung Walther König, 2014.

Ernst Bloch, *The Principle of Hope*, Volume 1. Trans. Neville Plaice, Stephen Plaice, and Paul Knight. Cambridge, MA: MIT Press, 1995.

Laurence A. Rickels, *The Case of California*. Baltimore, MD: Johns Hopkins University Press, 1991.

Paul Lafargue, *Le Droit à la paresse* (1883). Paris: F. Maspero, 1969. (An anti-work manifesto written by Karl Marx's son-in-law, born in Cuba of creole and mulatto parentage.)

Dean Allen, typographical design (poem titles). *Debbie: An Epic* (poems by Lisa Robertson). Vancouver: New Star Books, 1997.

Editors, graphic designers, and marketing specialists at Wesleyan University Press (and University Press of New England).

Kind thanks, as well, to editors of the following journals, in which poems by BLUNT RESEARCH GROUP have appeared: *Chicago Review, Gulf Coast, MAKE, The Offing, Public Pool, The Recluse*.

And special thanks to all the folks at Noemi Press, which published a chapbook selection of poems from "Lost Privilege Company" in March 2016

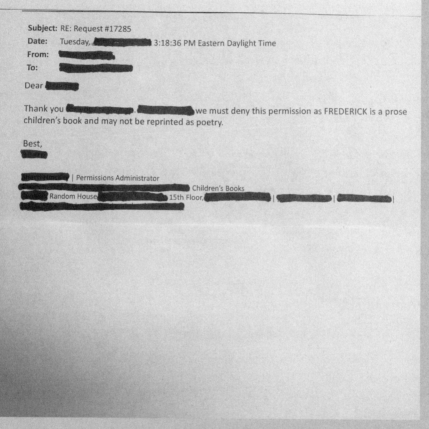

Subject: RE: Request #17285

Date: Tuesday, ▓▓▓▓▓▓▓ 3:18:36 PM Eastern Daylight Time

From: ▓▓▓▓▓▓▓▓▓

To: ▓▓▓▓▓▓▓▓▓

Dear ▓▓▓▓▓

Thank you ▓▓▓▓▓▓▓▓. ▓▓▓▓▓▓▓▓ we must deny this permission as FREDERICK is a prose children's book and may not be reprinted as poetry.

Best,

▓▓▓▓

▓▓▓▓▓▓▓ | Permissions Administrator
▓▓▓▓▓▓▓▓▓▓▓▓▓▓▓▓▓ Children's Books
▓▓▓▓ Random House ▓▓▓▓▓▓▓ 15th Floor, ▓▓▓▓▓▓▓ | ▓▓▓▓▓ | ▓▓▓▓▓ |

Figure 17. Denial of "Request #17285," seeking permission to quote passages from a classic children's book (for readers ages 3–7) about a little mouse named Frederick whose "work-shy" tendencies puzzle and anger his hard-working mouse family.

BLUNT RESEARCH GROUP is a nameless constellation of poets, artists, and scholars from diverse backgrounds. Collaborators on the current project include an esteemed Chicana historian, along with a troupe of scattered archivists, editors, designers, and translators. Drawing on historical examples of anonymous collectives in the arts (Situationist Councils, the Invisible Committee, Research and Destroy, "Karen Eliot" and the "open pop-star" idea), BLUNT RESEARCH GROUP presumes that poetry is by nature collaborative (in its common reliance on multiple sources), and it signals this orientation by using a collective signature, even as it continually tests and expands the premises of collaboration.

The decision to adopt the signature of BLUNT RESEARCH GROUP by clusters of individuals within the group for particular projects is determined by the sources, methods, and goals of each project. Work appearing under the signature of BLUNT RESEARCH GROUP need not always stem from direct or reciprocal transactions between multiple individuals, but the basic framework of its projects (and its collective signature) places in question the single-author function in the poetic tradition—a paradigm essential to maintaining systems of racism, class domination, and gender bias in literary culture. BLUNT RESEARCH GROUP seeks to re-activate and re-purpose the oldest poetic signature: *Anon*.

Wesleyan University Press
Middletown CT 06459
www.wesleyan.edu/wespress
© 2016 Daniel Tiffany
All rights reserved
Manufactured in the United States of America
Typeset in Garamond Premier Pro

Hardcover ISBN: 978-0-8195-7678-1
Ebook ISBN: 978-0-8195-7679-8

Library of Congress Cataloging-in-Publication Data available on request
5   4   3   2   1

This project is supported in part by an award
from the National Endowment for the Arts.